The Glittering World of Gems

RADIANT RUBIES

By Joseph Stanley

KidHaven PUBLISHING

Published in 2018 by
KidHaven Publishing, an Imprint of Greenhaven Publishing, LLC
353 3rd Avenue
Suite 255
New York, NY 10010

Designer: Seth Hughes
Editor: Vanessa Oswald

Photo credits: Cover (left) Bjoern Wylezich/Shutterstock.com; cover (right) TinaImages/Shutterstock.com; cover, pp. 1–2, 4, 6, 8, 10, 12, 14, 16, 18, 20–21, back cover (background) ILeysen/Shutterstock.com; p. 4 (ring) Popova Tetiana/Shutterstock.com; p. 5 (left), (right) Imfoto/Shutterstock.com; pp. 7, 9, 11, 13, 15 Thierry Falise/LightRocket via Getty Images; p. 12 (inset) NIK/Shutterstock.com; p. 17 DeAgostini/Getty Images; p. 18 (inset) JUSTIN TALLIS/AFP/Getty Images; p. 19 VCG Wilson/Corbis via Getty Images; p. 20 (top) Magnus Manske/Wikimedia Commons; p. 20 (bottom) Alex Wong/Getty Images; p. 21 (top) NATALIA KOLESNIKOVA/AFP/Getty Images; p. 21 (bottom) FABRICE COFFRINI/AFP/Getty Images.

Cataloging-in-Publication Data

Names: Stanley, Joseph.
Title: Radiant rubies / Joseph Stanley.
Description: New York : KidHaven Publishing, 2018. | Series: The glittering world of gems | Includes index.
Identifiers: ISBN 9781534523111 (pbk.) | 9781534523081 (library bound) | ISBN 9781534522985 (6 pack) | ISBN 9781534523012 (ebook)
Subjects: LCSH: Rubies–Juvenile literature.
Classification: LCC QE394.R8 S73 2018 | DDC 553.8'4–dc23

Printed in the United States of America

CPSIA compliance information: Batch #BS17KL: For further information contact Greenhaven Publishing LLC, New York, New York at 1-844-317-7404.

Please visit our website, www.greenhavenpublishing.com. For a free color catalog of all our high-quality books, call toll free 1-844-317-7404 or fax 1-844-317-7405.

CONTENTS

WHAT ARE RUBIES MADE FROM?

Rubies are shiny, red gems used in **jewelry**. These red crystals are formed from the **mineral** corundum, which is mostly made of the element aluminum. Another gem made from corundum is a sapphire.

A sapphire is blue because the corundum mixes with the elements iron and titanium. Rubies are red because they have chromium in them.

Mining for Facts!

Diamonds are the only gems that are harder than rubies.

Rubies are put in different kinds of jewelry, such as this ring.

Shown here are two uncut gems. On the left is a ruby, and on the right is a sapphire.

WHERE RUBIES ARE FOUND

Rubies can be found in many places. Some countries with large ruby **deposits** include Myanmar (also called Burma), Cambodia, and Thailand. The world's main source of gem-**quality** rubies used to be the Mogok Valley in northern Myanmar. However, now the area with the best ruby mining is Mong Hsu in central Myanmar.

Rubies are found close to Earth's surface. Miners find rubies by using tools to dig through rocks and dirt.

Mining for Facts!

Warriors in ancient Burma believed that putting rubies under their skin would keep them safe in battle!

Miners in Myanmar's Mogok Valley use tools to crush stones and find the rubies inside.

MINING RUBIES

One of the most popular ways to mine rubies is called open-pit mining. To do this, a miner digs a hole straight down. This hole is wider at the top and narrower as it goes down. Another way to mine rubies is to dig a tunnel. This is more work for miners, but it produces more gems.

In Myanmar, many of the ruby mines are small and worked by families. The ground is soft, which makes it easy for them to dig. As the miners dig through dirt and rock, they look for red-colored stone.

Mining for Facts!

Diamonds, emeralds, and sapphires are easier to find than rubies.

Shown here are miners in Myanmar digging a tunnel to try to find rubies.

DISCOVERING GEMS

Once dirt and rock have been dug up and put on screens, miners pour water over the screens to hopefully find gems. When the small pieces of dirt are washed away, the miners look closely at every stone. Only a few rubies are found in a day.

Ruby mines are often located near large sources of water, such as rivers. This is useful for miners because it takes a lot of water to rinse the stones from the ruby mines.

Mining for Facts!

A screen is a metal grid with a frame around it. Dirt passes through the screen, leaving larger stones behind.

This young girl is using a screen to hopefully find rubies!

RAW RUBIES

When a ruby is found, it's a raw and uncut six-sided crystal. These gems are formed for a long time deep inside Earth, where it's very hot.

While rubies form, small pieces of other minerals get trapped inside. These tiny bits of minerals are called inclusions, or flaws, and all rubies have them. Rubies with the fewest flaws are the most **valuable**. A ruby is bright red and **transparent** once it's cut and **polished**, which makes flaws easier to see.

Shown here is a cut and polished ruby.

A raw and uncut ruby can still be attached to a stone when it's found.

CREATING RUBY JEWELRY

Rubies are made into beautiful jewelry, but this takes a lot of work. First, a ruby is heat treated, which removes other minerals that were trapped inside it. This takes away many of the gem's flaws and makes it more valuable.

Next, the ruby is shaped with water and a diamond-tipped saw. Then, a jeweler called a lapidary **grinds** facets, which are small, flat sides, onto the crystal. After this, the ruby is polished and ready to be set in gold or silver. Small hooks called prongs curve around the edges of the stone to hold it in place.

This stonecutter is polishing a ruby in his workshop in Myanmar.

SPECIAL RUBIES

There's a special kind of ruby that looks a little different than the rest. This type of ruby is called a star ruby. It's different because when the light hits it, a star shape appears.

Star rubies are created from a small amount of the element titanium, which is a metal. The ruby is cut and polished into a smooth cabochon shape, which is round or oval. This shape shows off the star pattern the best.

Mining for Facts!

Most rubies set into jewelry are small stones. Larger rubies in jewelry are **rare**, which makes these gems really valuable.

Shown here is a star ruby with a bright and shiny star pattern.

THE VALUE OF RUBIES

There are many different features that decide a ruby's value. These are cut, **clarity**, color, and size. Color is the most important feature of rubies. A ruby can be bright red to slightly purple, but deep-red rubies are the most valuable.

Transparent rubies with well-cut facets that shine under light are also very valuable. Larger rubies with a higher carat weight are worth more, too. The weight of a gem is measured in carats. One carat is equal to 0.007 ounce (200 mg).

Mining for Facts!

The most expensive piece of ruby jewelry is the Burmese Sunrise Ruby ring, which sold for $30.3 million in 2015.

This necklace has many rubies and diamonds, which makes it very valuable.

FAMOUS RUBIES

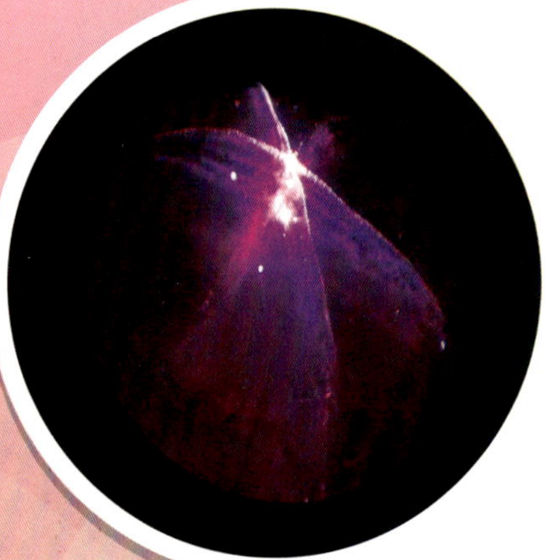

What: Rosser Reeves Star Ruby, which is one of the world's largest star rubies

When: Rosser Reeves, who the stone is named after, donated it to the Smithsonian National Museum of Natural History in 1965.

Where: found in Sri Lanka

Weight: 138.7 carats (27.7 g)

Value: $40 million

What: Carmen Lúcia Ruby, which is one of the world's finest large Burmese rubies

When: Businessman Peter Buck donated this gem in memory of his wife Carmen Lúcia to the Smithsonian National Museum of Natural History in 2004.

Where: found in the Mogok region of Burma

Weight: 23 carats (4.6 g)

Value: unknown

What: Richard Burton Ruby and Diamond Ring

When: Actor Richard Burton gave this ruby to actress Elizabeth Taylor in 1968.

Where: found in Burma

Weight: 8 carats (1.6 g)

Value: sold for $4.2 million in 2011

What: JAR Camellia brooch

When: This brooch was created for Lily Safra in 2003.

Where: unknown

Weight: 173 carats (34.6 g)

Value: sold for $4.3 million in 2012

Mining for Facts!

Ruby is the birthstone for the month of July.

GLOSSARY

clarity: The state of being clear.

deposit: An amount of a mineral in the ground that built up over a period of time.

grind: To shape or smooth something with a rough surface.

jewelry: Pieces of metal, often holding gems, that are worn on the body.

mineral: A natural, solid substance that is not a plant or animal.

polish: To rub something with a soft cloth to make it smooth and shiny.

quality: The standard of something.

rare: Not seen very often.

transparent: Easy to see through.

value: The worth of something.

FOR MORE INFORMATION

Websites

Gem Kids: Ruby
gemkids.gia.edu/gem/ruby
This website includes colorful illustrations and fun facts about rubies.

National Geographic Kids: Ruby
kids.nationalgeographic.com/explore/science/ruby/#ruby-raw.jpg
This website has cool photos and information on rubies.

Books

Callery, Sean, Gary Ombler, and Miranda Smith. *Rocks, Minerals & Gems*. New York, NY: Scholastic, 2016.

Harding, R.R., and R.F. Symes. *Crystal & Gem*. New York, NY: DK Publishing, 2014.

Publisher's note to educators and parents: Our editors have carefully reviewed these websites to ensure that they are suitable for students. Many websites change frequently, however, and we cannot guarantee that a site's future contents will continue to meet our high standards of quality and educational value. Be advised that students should be closely supervised whenever they access the Internet.

INDEX